MEDIEVAL ASPECTS OF OXFORD UNIVERSITY

by David EP Dennis

Volume 1

VACARIUS

AND THE

DEVELOPMENT OF CIVIL LAW

DOMI NVS ILLV MINA TIO MEA

Published in Great Britain

First edition published June 2023

All characters in this publication are factual and any resemblance to real persons, living or dead, is deliberate.

Image: The crest of Oxford University is taken from the public domain file of Wikimedia Commons.

Series Introduction

This series of books will examine a wide range of positive and negative connections between Oxford University in England, and the world in medieval times (c.1066-1500). How did people at Oxford's great seat of learning, by occupation or invitation, think - and what did they think about? What kinds of events happened in the area? What were the relationships between the monarch, religious leaders, local population, foreign institutions, and the university?

Contents

Chapter 1

Preface

Dear Reader

This book is the first in a series about Medieval Oxford and its university. This edition, Volume One, is about the relationship between Oxford University and the development of the law – especially the civil law although some early law merged civil and criminal aspects. There has always been some sort of rule, initially tribal, with some alpha male forcing a desired outcome through violence, or perhaps the whole tribe sitting down together to decide on the limits to freedom in order to ensure maximum cooperation for the benefit of all. From the earliest times there was punishment for law-breaking, with ***Lex Talionis*** – the Babylonian system of matching the punishment with the crime – an eye for an eye. In this book a range of laws enforced by kings and emperors are set out in simple wording so that you may see how simple and mostly harsh the early laws were. They were usually phrased – 'If...then...' If you have murdered then you will be killed' and so on.

The Advent of Civil Law

In England and in most of Europe over the period from medieval times to now, various kinds of laws, regulations and codes of behaviour or guidance have evolved. For example, Common Law, Criminal Law, Civil Law, Church Law, Canon Law, Decretals, Export Regulations, Byelaws, the UK Highway Code and Country Code, and so on. In this book we are looking at the idea of **Civil Law based on Roman Law**. This is different to **Common Law**. It is said that Common Law has developed from thousands of individual decisions by the early courts as to how to view crimes. These decisions over many years act as precedents, showing the way that judges and jurists think that the next identical or similar case should be dealt with. So for example, in Britain, the offence of murder is tried under Common Law, not Civil Law. In England the Crown Prosecution Service makes decisions on **Common and Criminal Law**, such as murder, rape, arson, burglary, theft, vandalism and other forms of violence or illegality against the person or their property. Trial is usually by judge and jury.

Civil Law is a developed set of codes of legal behaviours derived from Roman Law. These laws have been refined by expert jurists and reintroduced in a more modern fashion in medieval times via the early universities of Europe, to make decisions about, for example: marriage, civil partnership, the custody of children, bankruptcy, defamation (libel and slander), breach of contract, negligence resulting in injury or death, property damage and other private matters between individuals. Cases are dealt with in order to give restitution or for judges to give clarification as to how parties shall or must proceed.

We all want love and peace — time to develop our relationships, perhaps to bring up a family or to have adventures with partners. We cannot act in any psychopathic way we please without hazarding others. Our British and European civil law has evolved from Roman Law. So in this book I chart the gradual pathway from early attempts to set standards of behaviour and punishment, to more refined thinking by jurists attached to the early European universities. One brave and clever legal thinker who came from Italy to England and to Oxford University was **Vacarius**, and he is the main subject of this book. You may never have heard of him or the problems he faced, but I hope this book will remedy that to some extent.

Chapter 2

Introduction

In the beginning

Humans - the bipedal and highly intelligent Great Ape *Homo Sapiens* - emerged around 300,000 years ago in Africa. We evolved from a complex background of apes that succeeded and those that became extinct. From the way that stone tools were being used, and the use of fire, and the growth of cave art and bone carving, we assume that they were organised into family groups within larger tribal entities. We do not know what sorts of unwritten laws there were as tribal and family groups evolved but we can imagine that some limits to behaviour were set, and some co-operative rules did apply; punishment was swift. Many cases have been found of people strangled and left in bogs several thousands of years ago. For most of our early history, behavioural rules and customs have been taught verbally and by example by parents to children and by tribal leaders to tribal members. For several hundred thousand years therefore, no laws were written down, and all depended on mandate, custom and memory. It is a terrible truth that well before the first written laws, society was divided into humans and slaves. Slaves had few or no rights and suffered appalling hardship. Often, they had lost their rights because they had been defeated in battle. It is therefore deeply regrettable that the civilisation we have now was built on the suffering of slaves. No apology is sufficient.

Egypt

In the western hemisphere, when farming communities had been established, then law codes began to be written down around 3,000 BCE in Egypt. The rule of law was to ensure impartial social equality (apart from the thousands of slaves of course). The well-known story of the Israelites who escaped from Egyptian captivity and fled into the wilderness gives us a clear indication that slaves are people – humans who would risk everything to be free. Freedom is innate and paramount to humans. No formal written law code has yet been found for early Egyptian rule by pharaohs, however the World History Encyclopaedia describes the situation thus:

> 'Ancient Egyptian culture flourished through adherence to tradition and their

legal system followed this same paradigm. Basic laws and legal proscriptions were in place in Egypt as early as the Predynastic Period (c. 6000- c. 3150 BCE) and would continue, and develop, until Egypt was annexed by Rome in 30 BCE. Egyptian law was based on the central cultural value of *ma'at* (harmony) which had been instituted at the beginning of time by the gods. In order to be at peace with oneself, one's community, and the gods, all one had to do was live a life of consideration, mindfulness, and balance in accordance with ma'at.

Humans are not always considerate or mindful, however, and history illustrates well how poorly they maintain balance; and so laws were created to encourage people on the desired path. Since the law was founded on so simple a divine principle, and since it seemed clear that adhering to that principle was beneficial to all, transgressors were often punished severely. Although there are certainly cases of leniency shown to criminal suspects, the operative legal opinion was that one was

guilty until proven innocent since, otherwise, one would not have been accused in the first place.'

Sumeria and the Laws of Babylon

By 2,200 BCE the first Sumerian law code was written on clay tablets, and it emphasised the status of free men and slaves – the latter still being 'non-persons'. The oldest written code of law is that of Ur Nammu. It is from Mesopotamia, written on tablets in the Sumerian language around 2100–2050 BCE. Sumeria evolved into Babylon following invasion by the Akkadians. The **Code of Ur Nammu** was a sophisticated list of more than thirty rules with generally brutal punishments for crimes against society but with many minor offences satisfied by the payment of money. Here are some paraphrased examples:

- If a man commits a murder, that man must be killed.

- If a man commits a robbery, he will be killed.

- If a man commits a kidnapping, he is to be imprisoned and pay a fine in silver.

- If a slave marries a free person, he/she is to hand the firstborn son over to his owner.

- If a man violates the right of another and deflowers the virgin wife of a young man, they shall kill that male.

- If the wife of a man followed after another man and he slept with her, they shall slay that woman, but that male shall be set free.

- If a man proceeded by force, and deflowered the virgin female slave of another man, that man must pay a fine in silver.

- If a man divorces his first-time wife, he shall pay her some silver.

- If the man had slept with the widow without there having been any marriage contract, he need not pay any silver.

- If a man is accused of sorcery or magic he must undergo ordeal by water; if he is proven innocent, his accuser must pay a fine.

- If a man accused the wife of a man of adultery, and the river ordeal proved her innocent, then the man who had accused her must pay a fine in silver.

- If a slave escapes from the city limits, and someone returns him, the owner shall pay money to the one who returned him.

- If a man knocks out the eye of another man, he shall pay back in silver.

- If a man has cut off another man's foot, he is to pay a fine.

- If someone severed the nose of another man with a copper knife, he must pay him some silver.

- If a man's slave-woman, comparing herself to her mistress, speaks insolently to her, then her mouth shall be scoured with 1 quart of salt.

Around three hundred years later, in 1,760 BCE the famous **Codex of Hammurabi** set out Babylonian Law with its very clear wording cut into black stone obelisks called stelae. Common and Criminal Law were still mixed up with Civil Law on the same stelae. To paraphrase the detail of the law, here are some simplified Babylonian legal outcomes:

- If a man blinds someone, then he himself shall be blinded.

- If a man breaks into the house of another to steal, he shall be hanged in front of that house doorway.

- If a man accuses another of murder and cannot

bring proof of that accusation, the accuser shall be killed.

- If a slave says to his slave-owner, 'You are not my master.' and the slave-owner brings proof that this is false, then the slave shall have his ear cut off.
- If a child, for some reason, is adopted at birth by a person, then the original parents cannot claim it back.
- If a builder shall build a wall of a house and that wall then buckles, the builder shall use his own money to correct the fault.
- If an ox runs riot through the town and gores a man to death, nothing can be done and no-one is guilty.

The Transition from Greek to Roman Law

Later still, the Greeks set out the differences between Divine Law, Human Decrees and the Custom of the Land. These streams of law have merged to become eventually the basis of early Roman Law. When the Romans, in the early 3rd century BCE, took over Greece, a land renowned for the works of Homer and the famous philosophers Socrates, Plato and Aristotle, they came to admire their laws and culture and tried to emulate them. The Roman

State was legally pagan by definition until the **Emperor Constantine I's** Edict of Milan in 313 CE, when he ordered the empire to favour Christianity and cease persecution. Eventually in 380, the Roman Empire became fully Christian. It split into eastern and western divisions in 395. The western empire was plunged into chaos by repeated invasions. By this time there were many laws, some of them making little sense.

One of the divided empire's Eastern Emperors was **Justinian I**, who ruled from 527 to 565 and gathered together teams of jurists to revise the extant law into fresh legislation as you will read in greater detail below. As the old Roman Empire faded, then **Charlemagne** ruled the Empire of the Romans from 800 to 814 and eventually the Holy Roman Empire arose, using that title from 1254. It is important to remember that regardless of emperors and kings, the Holy Roman Catholic Church had popes who ruled all of Christianity. The Church did not split into western and eastern divisions until 1054 and the western schism which set Pope against Anti-Pope occurred from 1378 to 1417. All the emperors were crowned by popes, making for an almost unbreakable connection between Christianity and civil authority. The fine detail of the Christian religion and its dogma was studied in special schools of students such as at Padua, Italy. Both emperors and kings began to resent papal interference in the civil administration of their states. The political and religious turbulence was severe for many years, and this produced rival factions with great battles and many deaths.

The Laws of Charlemagne and the Suppression of Saxon Paganism

In the 9th Century it was necessary to become King of the Franks before being crowned by the pope as Roman Emperor. So from 771 to 814 Charlemagne ruled the Franks, and as emperor, from 800 to 814. As a devout Christian, he had many problems with the Saxons, who were pagan and worshipped Nature. That may sound admirable in today's climate change circumstances, however, back then the Saxons had some deeply unfortunate customs as you will see below. These customs were entirely legal to them and part of their natural civil and religious practice. However, Charlemagne issued a set of laws called **Capitulatio de Partibus Saxoniae** (Ordinances concerning Saxons) in 782 to suppress the horrific Saxon customs and force the tribes to become Christians on pain of death. Once again there was a mixture of laws – criminal, religious and civil.

Here are some of Charlemagne's laws simplified to aid better understanding:

- If you are a Saxon and try to hide yourself among Christians and yet you have not been baptized or have refused to come to baptism, I will have you executed.

- There are to be no meetings or legal trials on the Sabbath - the Lord's Day. You must go to church, then pray and listen to the preachers.

- Do not pervert the course of justice by giving gifts to overturn judgements. I will fine you and even if you are of high rank. You will be fined and you will also lose your status and position and be removed.

- If any of you join together in a conspiracy with other pagans, using trickery and fraud against me your king to try and oppose one or more Christians, I will arrest you and execute you.

- If you, while continuing the practise of worshipping trees, planted or natural groves, or springs and bodies of water, then make vows to demons in those places, I will fine you according to your rank. If you have no money to pay the fine, then you will have to work for the benefit of the Christian Church until the debt is paid off.

- Do not sacrifice any man to the Devil or pretend that he is required to be a victim of the demons, or I will have you executed.

- There are no witches, therefore if any Saxons con-

> tinue to act in a pagan manner and accuse any man or woman of being a witch, setting fire to them and eating them, or sharing their burned flesh in a communal cannibal meal with others, I will ensure that he is executed.

Irminsul and the Verden Massacre

In October 782, as these ordinances were being promulgated, Charlemagne ordered that c.4,500 Saxons be beheaded all in one day in order to prevent their continued worship of the Great Pillar or Irminsul, a giant carved tree in the shape of a man-like creature, in the sacred groves of the Saxons. This massacre occurred at Verden, at the confluence of the Aller and Weser rivers. Over the years historians have argued about this appalling ethnic cleansing which showed both Christianity and Charlemagne in a bad light. It raises the great questions – are we free to do as we will through wish, habit or custom - or does Man have an inalienable right to life and personal safety? Can a human lose their rights when enslaved? Charlemagne decided to execute humans because their law codes were different and yet throughout history Christians have been burning heretics for their beliefs. So many people have died terrible deaths before the law began to be clarified into what we call now, civilised society. Yet across the world, many countries still have laws that Charlemagne would have been dismayed by. There is still a long way to go to achieve global fairness and the 'Rights of Man'.

The Laws of William the Conqueror

In the medieval period from 1088, first the new university of Bologna, and then later Paris, Oxford and Cambridge evolved against a background of ecumenical laws set out by the popes of the Roman Catholic Church and traditional laws defined by kings and princes ruling their own lands. King William of England was also Duke of Normandy and he lived from1028 to 1087. His English laws were a basic mishmash of previous Anglo-Saxon land law and Norman law. When he pledged during the coronation ceremony in Westminster Abbey on 31st December 1066 that he would uphold the law, his fairly primitive list of ten laws was as follows:

- Above all things the King wishes one God to be revered throughout his whole realm, one faith in Christ to be kept ever inviolate, and peace and security to be preserved between English and Normans.

- Every freeman shall make an oath that he will be loyal to me, King William and protect my lands.

- The Normans that I, your Lord King brought with me shall have peace and if any of them is murdered then the Lord shall seize the perpetrator.

- Every Frenchman remaining in England shall pay local taxes and levies in the same way as the local population.

- A person can only sell cattle in a city if he has three credible witnesses that the herd belongs to the seller.

- If a Norman shall charge an Englishman with a crime, then the Englishman can defend himself in such manner as he prefers: with either a hot iron or a battle.

- People shall follow the old laws of King Edward the Confessor in respect to lands and possessions.

- Every man who wishes to be considered a freeman shall be made to make a promise or pledge so that his surety shall hold him, and hand him over to justice if he shall offend in any way.

- The sale of a man as a slave to anyone outside England will incur a fine payable in full, to me as King.

- No-one shall be hanged or slain for any crime. Instead they are to be blinded and castrated. If anyone violates this law then they shall pay a fine to me as King.

We now move on to consider the first university in Europe at Bologna, where our legal hero Vacarius first worked.

Chapter 3

The University of Bologna

In this chapter we learn about the development of the first European university – at Bologna, and the fear it generated. We also read about the development of the Universities of Padua and of Paris and the rediscovery of the Roman Laws of Justinian.

The University of Bologna was founded in 1088. Later, the Holy Roman Emperor **Frederick Barbarossa** (Red Beard – 1122-1190) granted the University of Bologna's Law School its imperial privilege in 1158 and permitted the students there to govern themselves. In the same way as the students of Oxford fled periodically from local violence, so too did the students at Bologna, where the town (now city) population attacked them. Some students and teachers fled in terror to Padua to start a new university. Padua is where the notorious and brave Marsilius of Padua (c.1275-1343) wrote his heretical tract, *Defensor Pacis* which cursed the incursions of the popes. This was a follow-on to some of the work by the poet and thinker, Dante, who also explained the need for monarchs to be able to rule despite papal edicts.

Paris

The University of Paris was given firm foundation by the King of France (Philip II 'Augustus') in 1200 (Hannam, 2009). These beacons of learning attracted both the religious and secular academics who wanted to know more about how the laws of church and state operated. Bologna specialised in evolving civil law by gradually replacing traditional laws with modified Roman law and canon law (the laws of the specific operation of the Roman Catholic Church). For the civil law at Bologna, the interest centred on replacing long-held customs and embedded traditional ways of dealing with crime and property with innovative ideas stemming from Roman Law of the Emperor Justinian who lived from 482 to 565 CE.

The Laws of Justinian

The jurists of Bologna and Padua became interested in the old Roman laws of Justinian. In his time, the Emperor Justinian I (482-565) decided to revamp the old Roman law system of his empire in the same way as we might sort out the mess in our house or flat. If we don't need it, throw it out. Then, if we have perhaps gone too far, add something back in again.

Justinian was born in Tauresium in the region of Dardania (Central Balkans) and said to be 'peasant stock'. However, he was bright and ambitious. He gathered together people learned in law, called jurists, and tasked them with examining the entire set of laws that applied at the time – around 529 CE, when he was about 47 years old. His face appears somewhat glowering and unshaven in the famous mosaic on the walls of St Vitale in Ravenna, Italy, although it is said that he never went there. The mosaic mural was set to overawe the people in a kind of 'Big Brother' way.

The jurists dutifully gathered together many old documents and also examined the writings of the much older Roman jurists to form what we now call the *Codex Justinianus* or **Code of Justinian**, although it was not called a code at the time. They made two works to show what existed then as law and what the old Romans thought about law. Then they produced four books because Justinian ordered the jurists to act as follows:

Codex Constitutionem – ten of you will examine every law made by previous emperors, remove all the oddities and things that no longer apply and rewrite the Codex to make sense now so that people can understand what their responsibilities and limits to action are. This was written in Latin and given out to the people in 529. Then in 534, when the proposed laws had a chance to bed down and were revised, Justinian formed a new commission of jurists to issue the final 12-book version of the Codex Constitutionem called *Codex Repetitae Praelectionis*. However, Justinian continued in his quest for valid laws.

Digest Pandectae – sixteen of you will form a commission and work between 530 and 533, working under the eagle eye of the jurist **Tribonian**. You will seek out all writings by all legal jurists, glean all the valuable aspects and make a decision as to what to say about each point so that there is absolute clarity. You may rephrase any law in order to make it clearer. Not only that but when you have finished, then you are to tell the people of my empire that all laws that are not now in your *Digest Pandectae*, are no longer valid laws and can be ignored. Write the law in Latin.

Institutiones – you are to obey the guidance of jurist Tribonian and produce an elementary Latin textbook so that those students new to the study of law can begin to learn how to apply the new laws.

Novellae Constitutiones Post Codicem – you are to set out some collections of rules and ordinances that I, Justinian have decided upon between 534 and 565. These will contain revisions and updates clear to all. Write this 'Novel' work in Greek and Latin.

Upon its formation, the new University of Bologna gathered together four great jurists who understood all that Justinian had ordered. They found all the old documents from hundreds of years before and began to interpret them. These famous jurists of Bologna were:

Bulgarus (c.1100-1167) – an outstanding legal mind.

Martinus Gosia (1100-1166) – his followers taught in southern France and became know as 'The Commentators'.

Hugo da Porta Ravennate (Birth date unknown and date of death around 1166-1171). Hugo wrote glosses named as *'Distinctiones'* and *'Summula de pugna'* and his students formed later schools that taught European rulers including William of Tyre.

Jacobus de Boragine (Birth date unknown and death c.1178). He examined and taught Natural Law and Equity.

Most importantly, it was **Irnerius** who was the teacher of these famous 'Four Doctors'.

Irnerius and our hero **Vacarius** probably worked together or at least knew each other. **We therefore look now at their works**.

Chapter 4

Irnerius

In this chapter we look at Irnerius, the Glossators and their Glosses

There was already a groundswell of change for the development of civil law which began in the 11th century. **Irnerius of Bologna** was born c.1050 (Britannica, 1911). As he grew in age and intellectual strength, he had heard of developments in the study of the 500-year-old Roman civil law at Pavia. Pavia seemingly had a law school dating back to the ninth century. This was very significant because there was already a deep question over the legality of the Pope to rule the Empire of the Romans. Emperor Lothair I was the power in Italy from 822 and when the Pope crowned him in 823, he demanded that the Pope acknowledge that he was subservient to the Emperor. Lothair's stance was to accentuate civil law. In fact, the University of Pavia, Italy says: 'Law has been taught in Pavia since 825, when the Holy Roman Emperor Lothair (795-855) established Pavia as the seat of a High School for students in law from Lombardy, Liguria and Piedmont.'

By the tenth and eleventh centuries, the Pavia school of law had developed great fame, not least for the very important collection of Lombard and imperial law known as the *Expositio ad librum papiensem,* meaning 'The Pavian Book'. This collection of laws is also know as the *Liber Legis Langobardorum* (The Lombards Book of Law). The manuscripts of these laws were written down between 1028 and 1039.

Then, at the Bologna in the 1070s, the first lectures on Roman jurisprudence were given by a consultant judge (*causidicus*) named **Pepo**. He had copies of the Laws of Justinian including the Code, Institutes and Digest sections of the work done by jurists under the watchful eye of Emperor Justinian hundreds of years before.

So it is clear that there was a groundswell or deep wish for the development of Civil Law separate to Church Law and also an ongoing rivalry between Emperors, Kings and Popes as to who was to be dominant and who subservient. Enter **Irnerius** who recognised that the seed at Pavia and Bologna for the new liberal arts study of civil law was the *Corpus Juris Civilis*, Codes, Institution Law and Digest of the Emperor Justinian I.

This shining jurist Irnerius (c. 1050– to after 1125), was given glowing praise as *lucerna juris* (lantern of the law).

Glossators

Irnerius founded the **School of Glossators**, around 1084-88, vying with another law school at Ravenna and updating Roman law to become applicable in his age as **Medieval Roman Law.** This was a deeply significant and explosive event. Non-ecumenical law, that is those legal aspects removed from anything to do with God, began to be set out in a more clear and structured form. These new 'civil' laws became understandable as a fresh way to civilise the population and gradually to remove the 'old law' that had been applied by the Anglo-Saxon, Norman and European church and state structures beforehand. Tremendous changes were on the way.

Encouraged by the **Margravine Matilda** (1046 – 1115) of Canossa in Tuscany, Irnerius set out the new jurisprudence in Rome and then in Bologna. At this time there was a great tension between the religious and secular powers – who had the right to set laws, the Pope or Kings? It was Matilda who brokered the peace and showed a relatively calm way ahead.

At Rome and then Bologna, Irnerius introduced a technique of teaching Roman law using glosses. Glosses were explanatory notes inserted into the text lines of the legal documents under study. Because there was much to explain, Irnerius started to write his glosses in the page margins as they would not fit neatly between the lines of text. This development became a regular practice.

Irnerius, upon the death of Pope Paschal II (1050

(55)-1115), was called upon to defend the rights of Emperor Henry V (1081(86)-1125 during the papal election and he gave legal rulings that antipope Gregory VIII (1100 (5)-1187) was the true pope. Because of this, it seems that Irnerius was taken into the court of the Emperor around 1116 and after Lothair III (1075-1137) became the Emperor, Irnerius died, around 1140.

Our man Vacarius, knew of Irnerius and his great work and may well have met him for discussions at Bologna. **So we now learn more about Vacarius.**

Chapter 5

Vacarius at Bologna

The Advent of Vacarius at Bologna

We now look at the work of the jurist **Vacarius** who taught law at Bologna and Oxford to rich and poor, and whose life ought to be better known. Perhaps the leading scholar on the life and works of Vacarius, is Jason Taliadoros, who stated that:

> **'Master Vacarius is no more than a shadow among the luminaries of the so-called twelfth century renaissance.'**

Jason Taliadoros 2006

The renaissance he alludes to is the new interest for England and Europe in 'law and legal science, the systematizing of theology and the flowering of universities' in the period after King William the Conqueror's Norman Conquest.

Cometh the Hour, Cometh the Man

Eben D Jacobs posted on the Internet in 2014: 'The origin of the phrase 'cometh the hour, cometh the man,' is not known. However, it's believed that it comes from the joining of the verse in John 4:23 'But the hour cometh, and now is,' and the English proverb; 'opportunity makes the man.' Certainly this man, Vacarius was a timely arrival for the evolution of civil law.

Vacarius (c.1120-1198/1200) was a travelling jurist, writer, lecturer and legal researcher who may have been born or lived in Mantua and is said more firmly to have come from Lombardy. He was certainly a gifted and provably brave intellectual who worked in Bologna, Italy to develop a very wide spectrum of legal thought. He examined the Laws of the Emperor Justinian and other laws to extract the best and most reasonable approaches to how people and states should conduct themselves less barbarously. He delved into the legal aspects of 'Marriage, Christology, Sacraments, Roman law, Canon law, Theology, Exegesis (critical interpretation), Logic and Philosophy' (Taliodoros, 2006).

Vacarius managed to dovetail theology and civil law

teaching as a 'scholastic' just as Greco-Roman culture was revived following the rediscovery of ancient documents, for example the works of Aristotle, mentioned above. (*Dictionary of National Biography* – Vacarius). Vacarius had such profound knowledge and perception that he was asked to act as a papal judge delegate during ecclesiastical work for both the Archbishops of Canterbury and York. His approximate contemporaries were **John of Salisbury** (1110-1180), **Robert of Torigny** (1110-1186) and **Gervase of Canterbury** (1141-1210).

He closely examined the real meaning of 'marriage' in his *Summa de matrimonio*, analysing the two extant models – consummation and consent, and reviewed divorce and the religious concept of marriage as a sacrament. He also dealt with heresy and the problems posed by the heretical statements of **Speroni**. However, one of his greatest achievements was to write a jurisprudence textbook *(Summa Pauperum de Legibus)* for Oxford University students specifically – popularly known as *Liber pauperum* which encompassed canon and Roman Law. (Taliadoros, 2006). It was modelled on the Summa *Codicis* of Irnerius who had taught at Bologna.

Vacarius came to England, perhaps in 1143, at the possible direct invitation of **Thomas Becket** (see below) with financial sponsorship from the Archbishop of Canterbury **Theobald of Bec**. He was awarded the prebend of Northwell at the college of secular canons at Southwell and also taught *Liber pauperum* at Lincoln in the 1170s and 1180s. He worked for **Roger of Pont l'Eveque** (c.1115-1181), the Archdeacon of Canterbury who became Archbishop of York from 1154 to 1181. Vacarius went to Paris in 1164 at the behest of Archbishop Roger, and along with Abbot Richard of Fountains Abbey, was asked by Pope Alexander III to decide a matrimonial lawsuit. He then went with his mentor Archbishop Roger to Aumale in 1171 because Roger had been summoned by the pope to face charges. Next, he witnessed the agreement between Roger and Hugh de Puiset, bishop of Durham, and, still busy, he was required to be judge-delegate in a controversy between Alan of Rydale and Rievaulx Abbey. Then he had to go to settle a dispute between the Priory of St Faith and the Priory of Coxford in Norfolk in 1175. His last work, in 1198 was connected to a crusade. Aged around 80 years old, he had to prepare a letter for Pope Innocent III to be used in the north of England and in this he was helped by the Prior of Thurgarten, Nottinghamshire. Then he fades from history. However, it can be proved that he cared for the poor as well as the rich and that in the case of *Liber pauperum*, he wrote a cutdown version of his work so that poor and less well-educated people might understand the law – an enduring and endearing act.

Taliadoros calls Vacarius 'the hermeneutic of the lawyer-theologian' and points out that:

'Vacarius applied the *ius commune* (European Common

Law) to theological and sacramental debates.'

As a result of student diaspora, copies or fragments of Vacarius' *Liber pauperum* exist at Worcester Cathedral Library, Avranches, Bruges, Prague, Kaliningrad, St Petersburg, Trier, and Oxford. His work on marital law can be found in Cambridge University Library. Another respected writer concerning the life and works of Vacarius is **Marcia Colish**, the President of the Medieval Academy of America and Visiting Fellow at Yale. Once again, **Taliadoros** has written in honour of her splendid work (Taliadoros, 2010) and he has discussed Vacarius and Speroni in relation to heresy, theology and didactic literature as well (Taliadoros, 2008).

We now move on to consider the evolution of Oxford University.

Chapter 6

Oxford University's Early Development

Early Oxford

In 1086, just before the University of Bologna was formed, Oxford had 1,018 houses and was the sixth largest town in England (Sager, 2005). Oxford University's origin as a formal collegiate seat of advanced learning and research began before 1096 as a community of religious houses - and by 1167 grew quickly, with a charter titled *Universitas Oxoniensis* in 1214, a Chancellor in 1224 – **Robert Grosseteste**, and a royal charter from King Henry III in 1248. Some Oxford students had fled from local strife to form the University of Cambridge and then, from previously established Halls of Residence, University, Balliol and Merton Colleges were formed at Oxford.

Oxford University was just one of several academic beacons that began to burn with a fervour for learning across Europe in medieval times, yet the quality of its discourse, the arrangement of its community and the courage of its leaders soon made Oxford into a university that attracted the finest thinkers from across the world. (Maxwell Lyte, 1886). Such thinkers included **Roger Bacon**, **John Duns Scotus** and **William of Ockham** (Sager, 2005).

There was also a community of academic and religious friends at Toledo in Spain where Jewish, Muslim and Christian scholars discussed Aristotle (Taliadoros, 2011) and translation took place (*Escuela de Traductores de Toledo).* Toledo was also famous for its Black Magic schools – seemingly every aspect of religion, nature and abomination could be discussed (O'Callaghan, 1975). For example, the satanist pirate Eustace the Monk learned his black arts there prior to settling in his operating base - Old Winchelsea in Sussex, England (Dennis, 2023 – *The History of Old Winchelsea*).

At the time of Oxford's early development, England had a class structure (still very much in evidence today), with a monarch and a 'ruling class' of lords and ladies in a House of Lords dating back to the Magnum Concillium or Great Council of the king's advisers in medieval times, and even the time of the Normans and before. The feudal lower classes were mainly ignorant of the detailed nature of the law because they could not speak Latin. Even now it is almost impossible for a person attending a Roman Catholic service to be able to debate the incredible intricacies of the dogma that define the sacraments. For most Roman Catholics, blind faith is all that is required. It is interesting to note that 'dogma' backwards can be written as 'Am God'.

Consequently, the Bible's wording was inaccessible to most feudal workers and their families who only spoke Middle English, and so the tenets of faith were explained to a greater or lesser extent and depth of understanding, by monks and priests. It would be hard for the laity to explain exactly why they had faith in what they professed to believe, because they did not own the learning but worshiped because they were told to, often on pain of death. They had little real idea of what was in the Old Testament or New Gospels because they could not read them. Later at Oxford, **John Wycliffe's** bravery helped to instigate the translations of the English Bible.

University Ferment

As noted above, the eventual University of Bologna (where I was born in 1946 when it was a World War II field hospital) preceded Oxford and was in early formation as a seat of learning by 1088. Oxford's learning potential increased when English students came back to Oxford from the University of Paris around 1167. The concept of a university as a place of high learning and discussion was growing, as Greek and Roman ideas modified by Arabic learning gradually spread through Europe to aid scientific and medical inquiry (see Dennis, 2022 – Deep Roots of the NHS).

Important discoveries concerning the works of Aristotle (*Corpus Aristotelicum*) and the Codex Justinian focussed the minds of academics at the University of Bologna. There was much communication between Bologna, Paris and Oxford. Vacarius of Lombardy taught at Bologna and brought his civil law teaching to Oxford. The key translator of Aristotle's work from the Greek was **William of Moerbeke** (1215 (35)-1286) who completed translation commissions for **St Thomas Aquinas** in order to have a fresh version to compare with the Syriac-based Toledo translations.

You can see the Dateline for these events after the References below.

Over the period of English university development, there existed traditional law, ecumenical law based on the Old and New Testaments of the Christian religion, canon law (the operating rules of the Church), and eventually a newly-develop civil law. The universities also paid close attention to the **Decretals** – the statements, sayings and writing of the Popes, and Papal Bulls – rulings concerning the exact criteria of faith that people should observe and the heresies that could destabilise the faith. These complex and swirling laws, regulations and guidance were written in Latin, and the arguments between kings, princes and popes caused much strife and bloodshed.

In medieval times, Christianity was deeply entrenched across the whole of Europe. Despite the words of toleration by **Jesus** to 'Love one another' (John 15:17), the Christian authorities used conversion or execution as their creed. As the Norman hegemony gradually became 'English', then in England, the medieval period was an exciting time for those interested in study, despite religious and political turbulence and the Black Death. Discussions and arguments were held on the works of St Augustine of Hippo (Augustinians), Pelagianism (Neopelagians) and St Thomas Aquinas and Averroes (Thomists), and also the nominalism that refuted Platonic universals. Remote popes and visiting cardinals decided what people could think and speak about. Students and teachers had to be careful not to fall into heresy and be excommunicated or have their works burned. They could be tortured and executed. During the medieval period also, the Roman Catholic Church held convocations to decide on policy – making lists of offences against the Holy Mother Church, which had a spider's web of control over kings and commons until the intellectual courage of those who had been at universities like Oxford shone through. They would not be silenced and eventually they won the day after many deaths.

Vital Intellectual Courage of the Universities

Despite the book-burning, across Europe a kind of 'foolhardy courage' began to leak out from the rigorous orthodox mainstream of belief. You and your works could be praised or burned at short notice and yet with great intellectual courage you stated what you thought or believed. When we consider football, we know we have a referee and rules - and breaking them could lead to a yellow or red card. Breaking the rules of the medieval church, meant that the Pope acted as referee and the red card was a pile of faggots. It is vital to have rules for sport. It is also essential to have dogma for religion, so that those who profess faith can understand, at least partially, what they believe to be true. However, the medieval church used inquisitorial torture and death instead of the love of Jesus to keep the ignorant faithful on track. They funded this cold narrowness using the sale of indulgences. You could even buy your dead relative an escape from Purgatory into Heaven if you had enough money. Universities were places where innovative free speech was at least attempted, despite the hovering satanic darkness of papal retribution.

There is a need for some understanding in this. It is necessary for all world religions to say what they believe and why. If you are a follower of a religion, you are expected to have faith in its leaders and the tenets of the religion. However, if you disagree with the religion and begin to speak out against it, then you become a heretic. With the Roman Catholic Church being such a massive and monolithic structure that ruled the lives of almost every person in Europe, there was no room for dissent or any kind of variance in thought that might overturn received dogma – and death waited in the wings for anyone foolhardy who spoke against it. In medieval times, the Christian faith was a harsh and bloody ultra-authoritarian thing. In the full sense of the word - it was fascist.

The idea of a university, where free discussion could take place regardless of civil or religious authority, was a superb development for civilisation. However, sometimes the free thought was met with violence and therefore thinkers had to be brave both intellectually and physically.

Greater intellectual freedom generated by the European network of universities

The development of universities such as Oxford, Paris and Bologna, the work of Irnerius and Vacarius and other thinkers, gave birth to a freedom pathway for English Church mystical literature, such as *The Epistle of Privy Counsel*, *The Epistle of Prayer* and *Dionysius' Mystical Teaching*, with Richard Rolle, Walter Hilton, and Julian of Norwich – and the remarkable and sadly unknown (possibly priestly) author of the *Cloud of Unknowing* who uses negation as a strategy to see through '*The Cloud*'.

In his introduction to the deeply mystical *Cloud of Unknowing* (one of my favourite books) Clifton Wolters (1978) says:

'The whole of the Western Church was quickened at

this time, France, Germany, Flanders and Italy all bear witness to the same profound stirring.'

Wolters mentions other religious mystics such as Mechtild, Gertrude, Angela de Foligno, Echart, Tauler, Suso, Catherine of Siena, Rysbroek and Thomas a Kempis and comments that all this took place amid the Hundred Years War, the Black Death, the Peasant's Revolt and the split Papacy between Rome and Avignon. By this I do not mean that Irnerius and Vacarius were mystics but that the communal nature of universities gave a kind of 'intellectual permission' for people to develop their own pathways – their written signature of thought.

What a wonderful thing it is to be able to state what you think out loud or on paper – to be free from tyranny, secret police, vindictive monarchs, psychopathic rulers and dictators and not have your brain crushed by knotted ropes. How much do we now have to cherish the bravery of people like Vacarius and those who followed in his footsteps.

We now move on to consider medieval law in more detail.

Chapter 7

Medieval Law at the time of Vacarius

Medieval Law at the time of Vacarius

Hue & Cry and Compurgation

To understand how different English law was in those far off days, here is a brief overview which sets out some of the problems that Vacarius would have known about as he began to influence English Civil Law, setting it aside from Common or Criminal Law.

All early human societies, regardless of their geographical separation or contact, developed laws to limit outrageous behaviour by advocating punishment. It seems to us today that some punishments were sensible and proportionate, such as fines, and some were draconian, such as being hanged, drawn and quartered. Certainly, from the earliest times in England there has been law and control, first by tribal chieftains and then by kings.

In late Anglo-Saxon England, the details of the *King and Structure of Society* are discussed in a University of Cardiff paper by Loyn (undated). The method of raising alarm and alerting to ongoing crime, and the duty for all villagers to lawfully pursue the probable culprit - called **Hue and Cry**, is described in a paper by Fordham University, New York (Sagui, 2013). Within the legal system of the King and subject to the rules of Hue and Cry can be found the concept of **Compurgation** from pre-Norman times, namely the time of Canute (reigned in England 1016-1035).

The Hue and Cry system was derived from Germanic ideas, originated in Kent, and became a widespread reality in England during the reign of King Athelstan (reigned 924-927), (Palgrave 1921). If a crime were committed the victim could (and must) summon their neighbours to shout and pursue the likely culprit. King Canute (a Viking) accepted this method as being legal. Furthermore – if anyone allowed a perpetrator to escape without shouting out and calling for help, then this could be considered a breach of the law and they could be fined. There were strict rules for Hue and Cry. They varied within and without the Danelaw, Wessex, and Mercia.

These rules were incorporated into the special devolved

courts of the Cinque Ports of southern England. Within the Cinque Ports was the town and major port of Old Winchelsea, a community of around four to six thousand people living on a shingle bank in the Rye Camber Bay, which was eventually destroyed by the sea in 1287. This community rebuilt on the sandstone heights of Petit Iham, the village of Winchelsea that is there today. Hue and Cry and Compurgation laws applied to the citizens of both Old Winchelsea and its cliff-top replacement.

Before there were police forces, Hue and Cry was an important method for societal protection. For example: West Saxon District (Palgrave, 1921 p.124/125)

> **'If anyone capture a robber or a thief, without Hue and Cry and pursuit from him who has suffered the theft and shall take his captive beyond the jurisdiction, he shall pay ten shillings for failure of arrest and at the next meeting shall hand him over to justice. But if he takes him beyond the next meeting of the court without permission of the Justice, he shall pay a forfeit of forty shillings.'**

Palgrave 1921

This alarm system was continued in the reign of Edward I in the *Statute of Winchester* in 1285 (Stubbs, 1870), just two years before Old Winchelsea was totally destroyed by the sea. So, once the culprit had been captured following Hue and Cry or immediate arrest, then the opportunity for compurgation followed.

Compurgation

Compurgation is a word that finally settled into that English form in the 17th century and was previously set out in Medieval Latin as *compurgatio* – from Roman Latin *compurgare* – meaning 'to purify entirely' or 'to purge'. However, the compurgation concept had been used by Normandy and France before 1066 and may even stem from law back in biblical times. No matter how guilty a person appeared to be, once *compurgatio* had been confirmed – they were utterly cleansed and therefore free of that particular crime, but could be accused of other crimes, of course. Despite its name origin, the first mentions (Potter, 2020 pps. 26-28) of such a system of law in England originated in Kentish Laws in the time of Hlothere (Old English *Hlophere*) and Eadric, dating to a charter of c.675. Potter comments extensively on it in his book.

Compurgation is a fascinating glimpse of how the medieval mind worked. No matter what offence had been committed, including theft and murder, it was possible to be set free under the lawful rules of compurgation when the Hundred Court sat. This book now shows examples of how this purification of the accused was conducted.

The Freeborh Law of Canute (Palgrave, 1921 p.167) states that:

'Every free man who will entitle himself to the privilege of compurgation and the protection of the *were* shall be included in the hundred.'

It is important to note that the '*were*' meant the value of a man's life (the worth). If the king accused him of a crime, the culprit might have to pay a fine – *wergild*. If a freeman was murdered then his relatives were entitled to his 'life value' or *wergild*, to be paid to them by the murderer (Molyneaux, 2015).

Furthermore, it was vital that every freeman 'belonged'; that is – he had to be included in a Hundred and a Tithing, as shown here.

The law continues in Canute's Secular Code (Palgrave, 1921 p.167):

> **'...and it is our will that every freeman be placed in a hundred and a tithing, whoever wishes to be entitled to clear himself, or to have a *wergild* price in case anyone proceeds to accuse him after he is twelve years old – and is not in a tithing, let him be thereafter no longer entitled to the rights of a freeman, be**

he householder or follower of another man. And let every man be brought in a hundred and under security, and let his surety protect him, and lead him to every right.'

Palgrave 1921

You may imagine that an officer of the court would say: 'Which tithing do you belong to?' and so in a sense, in those days, men were not free to transfer allegiance outside of the hundred and tithing system.

In the days of King Ethelred (*Unraed*, reigned 978-1013), when the Danish Vikings caused so much trouble in England, then the legal court of the Witan would ask for amends to be made for a freeman's offence (for example, breaching the fast, during national humiliation by Scandinavian oppressors) by perhaps paying a fine (Palgrave, 1921 p.737.)

Compurgation could also be used in civil cases not arising out of Hue and Cry. Palgrave goes on to say that:

'...in the Witan court of Kent, a certain Eadgiva must give proof "by compurgatory oath" by ordinary shire men, concerning the payment made by her father for the redemption of his land.'

What this compurgation meant was that the court would choose how many good and honest freemen would need to come and swear a purging oath, before the court was satisfied that justice had been done and the accused was cleansed of the crime.

Compurgation and Forgiveness – How Many?

The central question was – just how many men must take an oath? So in the case of one freeman (not a slave and not tied):

'If any man be appealed of theft and he be a free man, and if up to that time he had borne a good reputation and had witness to his probity, he shall purge himself (of his crime) by his own oath.'

For example: 'I am a freeman and I swear I did not do this.'

'However, if he has been convicted before, he shall purge himself twelve-handed.'

This meant that theoretically twelve freemen must freely swear an oath that the accused man did not do the crime. It seems that the number thirteen, being the number of Apostles plus Judas Iscariot was significant in this because the order of the court was that to purge oneself 'twelve-handed' one must find fourteen lawful men, chosen by name, to take the oath along with him. This avoided the dread number thirteen.

If the accused cannot find fourteen men by name who are willing to take the oath, then the accused can defend himself by the **ordeal of water or fire**. For example being plunged into cold water to sink or walking on hot coals or holding a red-hot iron bar whilst walking a fixed number of paces.

However, the victim/accuser also has to undergo compurgation because the court requires him to find by name seven lawful men who are willing to swear that the accuser is bringing the charge – not for malice or for any other reason except for 'what is right'. So the accuser's 'compurgation duty' was half that of the accused. Being an accuser had a higher status in law than a potential culprit. Being innocent until proven guilty was an idea whose time had not yet come. This system enhanced the possibility of false accusation leading to burning or drowning. Certainly, it also 'let you know who your friends are' to use a colloquial term.

Church Crime

The matter of compurgation escalates dramatically if church property is involved and in the case of a violating crime against a 'church' or 'house' (priory, monastery, abbey), then if the free man was previously blameless, a twelve-handed compurgation by oath was acceptable, in other words, fourteen men to swear his innocence.

But, in a huge escalatory compurgation, because an offence against a church or house was most serious (more so than any other part of society), then his required oath was tripled if he had previous convictions - and so he had to find not only the original twelve men but another thirty-six; so forty-eight men in all would have to be named and then swear an oath that he was innocent. If he could not find such numbers of men, he would have to endure (specifically) the ordeal by water. This might mean he was more likely to die by drowning than 'merely being agonisingly marked or disabled' by hot metal.

It is clear therefore that a previous conviction directly increases the likelihood that the person will suffer some sort of torment and probable death by drowning, unless he is guilty but exceedingly popular, capable of covert mass bribery, or so falsely accused that he deserves support by his companions, so that the law is not made an ass.

Land Crime

Where land ownership was concerned, the accused could not call on random strangers to swear that he was innocent – they must be men who lived on the land in question. When the accused was involved in some land-related crime, having previously been found guilty of any other offence, it must have been hard to find thirty-six men locally who would swear him free again.

Ship Crime

If a man was on board a ship and during a storm, he determined that the only way to save the ship and himself was to jettison the cargo, then he had to swear a *compurgatio* oath to the court that he did the action only to save his life.

Theft of Cattle or Sheep

In order to attempt a prosecution of a person suspected of stealing live goods, then the aggrieved owner had to find a warranter who would swear that the livestock did really belong to him. If a warranter could not be found then a bondsperson or the seller and witnesses to the original sale had to be found (Palgrave 1921, pps.134-135). It was important to prove that the owner of the livestock did know the bondsperson or warranter, even though they may be dead. But if they could not be found, or shown to have existed, alive or dead, then compurgation was achieved by his own oath and that of witnesses. The owner had to hand to the court six times the value of the loss as a returnable surety. Then finally if he could prove by three quarters of all the people living in his neighbourhood that the missing beast was of his own rearing, then he would win his case. Medieval law states:

'Because it has been decided on the strength of sworn testimony, it cannot according to English Law be upset.'

Obviously here, the 'neighbourhood' would be of variable size depending on the findings of the court and the number of people living there would also be variable (for example, farming on the edge of remote, hillslopes, marshes or dunes), so justice would be different from place to place. During the Black Death, justice by compurgation became almost non-existent for neighbourhood populations, with maybe only two or three people left alive in a village.

Robbery and Murder

We now come on to robbery and murder. The law set out that if anyone killed a Frenchman (or Norman) and the men of the neighbourhood did not capture and arraign the murderer within seven days, then the neighbours (collectively and apportioned individually) must pay a fine of forty-seven marks. A mark was 66.6% of a pound. So that would be a fine of say, £32.00, which in 1209 was proportionally worth the truly massive and financially withering amount of £52,569.00 according to the current Bank of England Inflation Calculator (earliest calculator date available 1209). It may be that this law against the murder of 'Frenchmen' was because of the disproportionate vengeance that would follow when the French found out and came to burn Hastings and Winchelsea and kill their inhabitants – which they did many times.

Real Cases of Compurgation (Palgrave, 1921)

Lastly, here are two real cases, described out of date order because the crime of the second date is less serious than the first date.

An example of *Compurgatio* for theft at the Hundred Court at New Winchelsea, Sussex

The Hundred is a term with a complex and distant origin. It may have referred to one hundred hides and sometimes was called *wapentake*. It seems to have been a county division. So a Hundred Court could be a county court, but in this case, it is used as a town court within the Cinque Ports legal system. Old Winchelsea had existed and developed on a huge shingle bank in the sea area called The Camber, between Pett and Broomhill, south of Rye, Sussex from around 900 CE until it was swept away by a great storm in 1287. The laws of the Cinque Ports applied to Old Winchelsea and that included Compurgation. So the Hundred Court system was continued after 1287 at its new location.

The replacement of Old Winchelsea, which had been beset by great storms since 1250, was ordered by the King who sent his Treasurer down to the port to plan the building of a new town on the heights. New Winchelsea was then built on the sandstone heights of Petit Iham.

Although there will have been many cases before, the first case mentioned by Palgrave of *compurgatio* in the Winchelsea Hundred Courton Petit Iham heights occurred in the year 1441 on the 5th of February. The mayor acting as judge at the time was Godard Poulham. The bailiff, William Pope, was absent but the available bailiff's deputy was Thomas Selton. The jury was Roger *ate* Gate, John Godfrey, Thomas Thundir, William Allard (sic) (from a well-known pirate family – the Alards), Richard Richorn, Thomas Wodeward, John More, John Kynth. From this list it appears that ten men sat in judgement – not twelve – at least, the other two names are not known.

The accused was the Winchelsea barber called John Thomas. He had previously been arraigned for robbery –

namely 'the spoliation and felonious carrying away, on the 30th of the previous December of certain goods belonging to John Peris of Sandwich, a chapman (itinerant dealer or hawker).'

Now these goods were of significant in value. They were:

'A pendant called '*The Lamb of God*' made of silver gilt, five crucifixes of silver gilt, eleven rings of silver gilt and twelve pence sterling, to the total value of twenty-six shillings and eight pence' – worth today c.£2,500.00.

When the Hundred court heard this charge they ordered John Thomas, having been convicted of a previous offence, to bring before the court on the 26th of February, thirty-six good and lawful men who could be his neighbours within the Hundred of New Winchelsea, to swear that he did not steal the goods, in which case 'he would be absolved forever of that charge'.

Unfortunately, the record does not state if he was able to find enough men to swear the compurgatory oath. The system obviously raises many questions. Was bribery involved? Can you pay enough people to swear the oath before God and the court? Even though the jury of twelve men (supposedly) would find the man guilty, then thirty-six men could swear he was not, and he would be forever, free. I have assumed that because the record does not show that thirty-six compurgation oath-givers attended, that most probably John Thomas was drowned or burned with an iron bar.

New Winchelsea – the Second Case

The second case involves Agnes Archer who on the 24th ^{of} April in the 13th year of King Henry VI (1 September 1434 -31 August 1435) had already been indicted by twelve good and lawful men who had sworn an oath before the Mayor of Winchelsea at that time, namely William Fynche who was also the King's Coroner.

They wanted to know just how the poor victim Alice Colynbourgh, had met her death. Alice had been found dead within the franchise of Winchelsea. So Agnes was brought before the court by the court serjeants. She was bare foot and bare-headed and with no outer garments (not naked but with a simple shift). Her hands were bound. She was made to raise her right hand when the rope was removed.

The indictment was read out:

'That on the seventh day of April you committed a felony in that you robbed Alice Colynbourgh of six spoons of silver worth twelve shillings sterling, and a gyrdylle harnessed with silver worth six shillings and eight pence, and also of five shillings of silver within Alice's purse in a Strand called Trecherye.'

'Further that you, Agnes then murdered Alice by stabbing her in the throat five times causing her to be dead. How do you plead?'

'Not guilty of these deeds, I have done ney none of them

so help me God.'

'How will you then acquit yourself?'

She answered that she would acquit herself by compurgation in which 'God and the neighbours of the town' would be called as witnesses to her innocence.

The court then told her that if she did want to acquit herself, she must name thirty-six men and bring them to the court from anywhere within Winchelsea Hundred franchise. Presumably, God was not immediately available.

Then Agnes asked the Mayor:

'May I now bring thirty-six men from the franchise within the town to swear upon oath that I am innocent?'

and the court said 'Yes'.

Agnes then said:

'I owe neither scott nor shilling, penny nor penny's worth. All that I have contracted to do I have performed.'

Once again, we do not know if Agnes escaped punishment, but it does seem, once again unlikely that she avoided death or mutilation.

We now consider the connection between Thomas Becket (the eventual Archbishop of Canterbury) and Vacarius.

Chapter 8

Thomas Becket

In this chapter we look at the actions of Thomas Becket (1119-1170) as a student and then as Chancellor and finally as an Archbishop.

Becket was influenced in a circuitous way by thinkers from before the Norman Conquest and after it. However, in order to understand the link between Becket and Vacarius and how Vacarius began to affect the understanding and novel provision of civil law for England, we need to remember once more, the work of the Italian jurist, Irnerius (1050-c.1125) who came before him. We have already seen something of Irnerius in Chapter 4.

The *History of the University of Oxford* by H. C. Maxwell Lyte was published in 1886 and contains useful information on civil law developments at Oxford. Maxwell Lyte states that:

'The lectures of Irnerius at Bologna at the beginning

of the 12th century had done much to revive in Italy the long-neglected study of Roman jurisprudence.'

Students came to Bologna from far and wide and among them was Thomas Becket (c.1119-1170) who brought his learning from the lectures of Irnerius back to England.

Maxwell Lyte states that:

'No attempt was made to teach Roman Civil Law in England before the election of Theobald, Abbot of Bec (1090-1161) to become Archbishop of Canterbury.'

This appointment can be dated to c.1138. So how did Becket become involved in the work of Irnerius? Becket had studied at the University of Paris when he was twenty years old but did not cover canon or civil law there and his Latin skills were relatively poor. However, when his father, Gilbert (*Beket*) suffered financial distress, Becket managed to obtain a living by working for Archbishop Theobald of Bec at Canterbury (although there is no suggestion that being called Becket to Theobald of Bec elicited some fruitful onomatopoeic connection).

Theobald recognised his potential for learning and gave him experience by sending him on horseback to Rome on missions and then to Bologna and Auxerre to study **canon law** in 1154 where he most likely read some or all of the civil and canon law works that Irnerius had delivered between 1084 and 1088 at Bologna. Once Becket had achieved the required learning, he demonstrated intellectual brilliance and was appointed Archdeacon of Canterbury and within a year, his meteoric rise led to Theobald recommending him as Lord Chancellor of England to Henry II. He attained this great office of state in January 1155. Archbishop Theobald died in 1161.

Yet things moved far too fast and led to ruin and horror. Remarkably, Chancellor Becket was ordained in the Roman Catholic priesthood on 2nd June 1162 and consecrated as Archbishop of Canterbury the very next day, a deeply unfortunate, frankly ridiculous accelerated promotion that effectively precipitated his dramatic change of attitude to the king and causing his almost inevitable downfall and savage death. On 29th December 1170, four knights cut off the top of his head and spilled his brains onto the floor of Canterbury Cathedral. Those knights had heard the king's remark: 'What miserable drones and traitors have I nourished and brought up in my household, who let their lord be treated with such shameful contempt by a low-born cleric?' This was converted later in the 17th century to the now more popular: 'Who will rid me of this troublesome priest?'

His assassination was said to be because of his implacable attitude for the preservation of papal authority over England despite the king's wishes. Even now in 2023, many historians gasp at the way that Becket changed roles and attitudes to the law so fast as though he had been 'reprogrammed' like some robot.

The Christian Bible's New Testament Gospel according

to St Mark is no help to an archbishop:

'And Jesus answering said unto them, Render to Caesar the things that are Caesar's, and to God the things that are God's. And they marvelled at him.' Mark 12:17

The obvious problem is – what belongs to God and what to the king? To answer this you first have to have faith that God exists in reality rather than a faith concept. As John states in his New Testament Gospel at 1 John 4:12 - 'No man has seen God at any time.' The book, **'The Cloud of Unknowing'** also explains this great mystery. However, an Archbishop knows that the king certainly exists in reality. The two can stand face-to-face. Any archbishop would consider that Papal Authority was the direct property of God. Only Common and Civil law could belong to the king - not Church Law. On the other hand, monarchs might think that since 'No-one has seen God at any time', then anything that happened anywhere in the realm and regardless of form or meaning, was entirely a matter for local decision. You might think that a country is ruled by a monarch not a pope. Since no-one has seen God, faith is required for belief in his existence, but no faith is required for belief in the existence of a king.

However, the king discovered that over one hundred murders had been committed by clerks (clerics, priests, monks etc) since 1154 and that many more cases of theft and robbery existed. These clerics had been tried by church courts only. This was intolerable to the king. This led to a series of incidents between church and state – known now as 'Becket and the Criminous Clerks.'

Part of the problem of religious or civil jurisdiction was clear well before Becket was made Archbishop of Canterbury. His promoter and predecessor, Archbishop Theobald of Bec, who was also the sponsor of Vacarius, had been involved in a dispute with King Henry II that had 'spilled over' from the reign of his predecessor, King Stephen. The courtier Osbert of Bayeux, sanctified priest and Archdeacon of York was accused of trying to poison the Archbishop of York, William – in effect, attempted murder and surely a common law crime. To ensure maximum leniency, however, Osbert tried to ensure that his alleged crime be tried in an ecclesiastical court and not in front of the king as a civil matter. King Henry told Archbishop Theobald that this move to thwart natural civil justice was unacceptable. In order to ensure that the Pope understood why the king had intervened, Theobald told him that it was the normal custom in England for clergy to receive judgement in secular courts.

An important example of the king's understanding of 'the customs, liberties and privileges...and of other things which ought to be observed and maintained in the realm', is set out in the book, *Law, Liberty and the Constitution* by Potter. One part of what was then called the 'Constitutions' stated that:

'Clerks cited and accused of any matter shall, when summoned by the king's justice, come before the king's court to answer there concerning matters which shall seem to the king's court to be answerable there, and before the ecclesiastical court for what shall seem to be answerable there.'

This meant that it was the king's court that decided which type of justice would be applied in which jurisdiction. Potter points out that a royal official would be present to observe the ecclesiastical court's work and that if found guilty, the miscreant would be returned for punishment administered by the royal court, not the church court. The pope plainly did not agree with local English tradition. The clergy had to be specially protected as they were chosen by God.

Archbishop Theobald therefore managed to assure the king that it was right and proper for an ecclesiastical court to take precedence. However, Osbert tried to obtain witnesses that he had never put poison into the Holy Chalice of the Mass to kill his archbishop, but failed. Not one monk or religious person came forward to side with his version of events, so the whole case was sent to the pope and because the 'turnover' of popes was quick, then Osbert appeared in front of two popes and still no judgement was made – at least, none has ever been found. This case highlights the real problem of medieval times – treating religious persons as being non-secular. At the time, it would have been normal to sentence someone to trial by fire. But Knowles says in *Cambridge Historical Journal* pp. 175–176 with regard to "Case of Saint William of York" that the Bishop of Hereford, Glibert Foliot reminded the pope in writing that the Archbishop of York had offered to prove his accusation by suffering trial by ordeal; this was not possible as the Church's canon law stated that **no clergy could be sentenced to any kind of ordeal.**

This brings us once more to the mention of **Compurgation** as it involved clerics. This was mentioned earlier in the previous chapter of this book, however, here is a reminder of the incredible level of church protection.

The matter of compurgation escalates dramatically if church property is involved and in the case of a violating crime against a 'church' or 'house' (priory, monastery, abbey), then if the free man was previously blameless, a twelve-handed compurgation by oath was acceptable, in other words, fourteen men to swear his innocence.

But, in a huge escalatory compurgation, because an offence against a church or house was most serious (more so than any other part of society), then his required oath was tripled if he had previous convictions - and so he had to find the original twelve men but also another thirty-six; so forty-eight men in all would have to be named and made to swear an oath that he was innocent and if he could not find such numbers of men, he would have to endure (specifically) the ordeal by water. This might mean he was more likely to die by drowning than 'merely being agonisingly marked or disabled' by hot metal.

It is clear therefore that a previous conviction directly increases the likelihood that the person will suffer some sort of torment and probable death by drowning, unless he is guilty but exceedingly popular, capable of covert mass bribery, or so falsely accused that he deserves support by his companions, so that the law is not made an ass.

To an extent, Vacarius helped to differentiate between the aspects of society that were religious and those that were civil. Inevitably there had to be a territorial battle to see which aspects of life were truly holy and which prosaic and ordinary. So many people died horrific deaths while the intellectual battle was fought out. Vacarius successfully walked the tightrope of law and dogma, and because of his brilliance, the interface between religious and civil matters became less complicated. It seems that Vacarius was a better man than Becket.

However, as well as Thomas Becket from England, Archbishop of Canterbury Theobald invited several foreign jurists to attach themselves to his English retinue and the chief of these was the learned Vacarius, who, as we have seen, had similarly studied the works of Irnerius and who undertook to teach what he had studied and taught at Bologna. In fact the Dictionary of National Biography of 1885-1900 suggests (as mentioned above) that Vacarius may have met Irnerius and listened to him orate. Furthermore, the Dictionary suggests that even though Archbishop Theobald may have been the formal sponsor of Vacarius, then maybe it was Becket who initially 'head-hunted' Vacarius to Oxford as a result of his trip to Rome to see Pope Celestine (died 1144) in 1143. Archbishop Theobald needed books on a range of laws to wrest the legateship from Henry of Blois (1096-1171), bishop of Winchester (the king's younger brother).

There was a great intellectual commotion when Vacarius began to teach in England and large numbers of students flocked to Oxford University to absorb the new civil law ideas. Vacarius then in 1149 made detailed extracts of the Codex Justinian, specifically the Code and Digest. Maxwell Lyte states:

'This alarmed **King Stephen**. He could not accept the rapid progress of such study which threatened to undermine the old laws of the realm.'

To understand this comment we need to remind ourselves of the mental stance of King Stephen. His predecessor, King Henry I, died on 1st December 1135 and King Stephen was crowned on 22 December of that year. He began to appraise himself of the kingdom's situation and especially who was loyal and who was a traitor. In 1137 King Stephen came to Oxford and held a council in which he ordered the seizing of the castles of men he perceived as traitors, for example, Bishop Roger of Salisbury. **The Anglo Saxon Chronicle** gives a true flavour of medieval times and the dire need for enforceable and fair law when it describes how Stephen was regarded by the traitors as so weak that they could do anything they pleased, and chaos ruled the land. Here is the grim and sorry tale:

> 'When the traitors perceived that he (King Stephen) was a mild man, gentle and good, and did them no justice, they all wondered. They had done him homage and sworn him oaths but they held not troth (real and practical pledged loyalty and fidelity). They were all forsworn and their oaths abandoned, for every powerful man made his own castles and then held them against the king. They filled the land full of castles. They oppressed the wretched men of the land hard, with work on the castles, and when the castles were made, they filled them with devils and evil men. Then they took the people they believed had any goods, both by night and by day, men and women, and put them in prison; they were after gold and silver, and so tortured them with unspeakable tortures, for never were martyrs tortured as they were. Men hung them by the feet and smoked them with foul smoke. Men hung them by the thumbs, others by the head, and hung

byrnies (chain mail hauberks) on their feet. Men put knotted strings about their heads and twisted them so they went into the brain. They put them in prisons with adders, snakes and toads therein, and killed them thus. Some they put into a *crucethus*, that is, a chest that is short, narrow and shallow, and put sharp stones therein, pressed the man therein and broke all his limbs. In many castles were *lof and grin*, that is, chains that two or three men had enough to do to bear one, so made that it is fastened to a beam and a sharp iron done on around a man's throat and his neck that he might not move from there any way, neither sit not lie nor sleep, but bear all the iron. Many thousands were killed with hunger.'

Anglo-Saxon Chronicle translated by Anne Savage

Plainly, for some living in medieval times, life was dire. People were trapped into subservience by their lords and the required and onerous 'loyalty' and 'fealty' they had a duty to show. They also had to be obedient to the Pope and the tenets of the Roman Catholic Religion or be burned as heretics. Vacarius had to take all this into account when explaining how Roman jurisprudence could be adapted to replace the old traditional laws of England. Not only that but he had to overcome the concerns of King Stephen that the 'old ways of justice' were still fair. So Vacarius tried to convince conservative King Stephen that it was time to move on to Roman Civil Law.

Burning Issues

King Stephen now began a programme of repression against Vacarius. Instead of consulting with Vacarius to set in train a programme of improvement of the law, King Stephen ordered him to cease his lectures. **There followed a royal edict forbidding any Englishman to own a treatise on foreign law.** Then the burning of the manuscripts began amidst a time of maximum repression at Oxford. If nothing else this showed the power of Oxford's intellectual achievements against a deeply apprehensive king. However, Vacarius may have thought that God was on his side because King Stephen died on 25th October 1154 of 'stomach disease', with Archbishop Theobald by his bed.

While Thomas Becket was studying in Bologna, Henry II became king. It is likely that the brave Vacarius remained at Oxford and certainly the university stood its ground, 'despite the fury of kings and popes' (Maxwell Lyte). Because of his persistence, Vacarius made the civil law a recognised and approved area of study for all at Oxford who wished to qualify in it.

Maxwell Lyte states that the newfound confidence in civil law studies helped to broaden the legal field 'with the introduction of **English Canon Law** based on the *Decretum* of the monk **Gratian.**'

Here we have to be careful because of the number of 'Gratians' in early history. The Gratian who lived from 359-383 CE had, with others, made Nicene Christianity the only legal religion in the Roman Empire and other religions and beliefs including non-Nicene worship became heresies. English Canon Law broadly met the Nicene criteria. Then there was Giovanni Graziano (John Gratian) who became Pope Gregory VI (died 1048). Beware the Wikipedia cross-hyperlink errors in the area of 'Gratians'.

However, the *Decretum* that Maxwell Lyte specifies was made by a monk called Gratian, (known as ***Gratianus clusinus episcopus***), a father of the study of canon law, who was probably born at Carraria-Ficulle in Tuscany and died before 1159. He may have been a jurist and rubricator (person who marks up emphasis in text using red ink) of the ecclesiastical forum at the monastery of Saints Felix and Nabor in Bologna. Certainly, he was a magister there (Britannica). In 1140, he wrote the treatise *Concordia discordantium canonum* to harmonize all the sources and remove all the contradictions that had occurred up to the Lateran Council of 1139. His canon law collection of rules has never been fully accepted into the Roman Catholic Church in its original form, but it did stimulate debate and study, especially at Oxford.

This Magister Gratian was grateful to the doctors of civil law at Bologna for a model used to set out the treatise in which he used Roman law and ecclesiastical law as well. It lasted so well that it was not extensively modified until 1917 and finally revised as part of official Vatican codification in 1983.

The implications of this civil law revision meant that traditional law would be gradually overturned by ways of doing things that evolved 500 years before. Not everyone was content and in England, King Stephen (1092 (or 96)-1154) tried to stop this progress. King Stephen of England's troubled reign lasted from 1135 to 1154. His rule relied on traditional laws that had been followed by Anglo-Saxon and then Norman kings.

Of course there were courts of law dealing with civil and ecumenical matters prior to the formation of Oxford University, but these used traditional legal rules. For example, Wikipedia sets out well the rigorous legal attitude of Henry II (1133-1189) after the death of King Stephen:

> 'In 1163 Henry returned to England, intent on reforming the role of the royal courts. He cracked down on crime, seizing the be-

longings of thieves and fugitives, and travelling justices were dispatched to the north and the Midlands. After 1166, Henry's exchequer court in Westminster, which had previously only heard cases connected with royal revenues, began to take wider civil cases on behalf of the King. The reforms continued and Henry created the General Eyre, probably in 1176, which involved dispatching a group of royal justices to visit all the counties in England over a given period of time, with authority to cover both civil and criminal cases. Local juries were used occasionally in previous reigns, but Henry made much wider use of them. Juries were introduced in petty assizes from around 1176, where they were used to establish the answers to particular pre-established questions, and in grand assizes from 1179, where they were used to determine the guilt of a defendant. Other methods of trial continued, including trial by combat and trial by ordeal. After the Assize of Clarendon in 1166, royal justice was extended into new areas through the use of new forms of assizes, in particular *novel disseisin*, *mort d'ancestor* and dower *unde nichil habet*, which dealt with the wrongful dispossession of land, inheritance rights and the rights of widows, respectively. In making these reforms Henry both challenged the traditional rights of barons in dispensing justice and reinforced key feudal principles, but over time they greatly increased royal power in England.'

We now move to our Conclusion.

Chapter 9

Conclusion

Conclusion

Unfortunately there does not seem to be sufficient information to show at which Oxford college Vacarius' civil law lectures took place. My guess is Merton. In fact there are still one or two academics who do not accept that he ever went there. It is rare that historians agree. However, in this book I assert that he did go to Oxford to help poor students. What is known is that the clerics of Oxford were under the jurisdiction of the remote Bishop of Lincoln and did not fear interruption by the local Prior or Abbot.

Thanks to the universities and the men and women who thought and taught there, our laws have become less primitive and more fair. There are now very sophisticated court systems and many Acts of Parliament readable by everyone online. Barrister Harry Potter (Selwyn College, Cambridge) has set the scene for the evolution of our

Constitution in his book, *Law, Liberty and the Constitution* (2015) and Matthew Lockwood has described the evolution of the **Coroner's Service** in his book *The Conquest of Death, Violence and the Birth of the Modern English State.* However the teaching of law in secondary schools is vital for the general understanding of what is permitted and what is unacceptable to society and the link at reference shows some of what is being done to teach law to young people. There is still much to do to improve law in England as new circumstances arise. The Law will never be perfect or accepted by everyone. The relations between the courts, the police, magistrates, barristers and solicitors, the Crown Prosecution Service and the government are turbulent and imperfect. Yet, this is the system we have and it is a great improvement on Codex Hammurabi, the Laws of William the Conqueror, Hue and Cry, Compurgation, drowning, hot coals, burning metal and hanging, drawing and quartering.

A Good Man

So what picture can we form of such a man as Vacarius? He seemed to be a brilliant teacher of the law, well respected, popular with students, kind and understanding to the poor, willing to help settle ecumenical and civil disputes. He was capable of good horsemanship, travelling long distances on horseback over mud-filled roads, putting up with variable comfort in a range of hostelries and probably a good sailor on his many cross-channel shipping trips.

He no doubt arranged packhorses to carry his books to Oxford. He probably spoke Greek, Latin, Middle Italian and Middle English and had a captivating voice, pleasant but determined manner and a celibate lifestyle. He was a civilian, not a priest but is mentioned many times in papal correspondence as *Magister Vacarius*. I think that if he appeared at Oxford today, modern students would flock to him and give him profound respect as a wise and kind teacher who opened people's minds.

I hope you have enjoyed reading this overview of the work of **Vacarius at Oxford** and elsewhere.

Volume 2 of this series examines the devious and serial attempts to assassinate King Henry III near Oxford.

Kind regards

David EP Dennis BA (Hons) FCIPD LCGI RAF

Associate Fellow of the Royal Historical Society

1st June 2023

Chapter 10

References

Dennis (2022):

Academia Paper 5 Destruction of Old Winchelsea 1287 FInal | David E P Dennis - Academia.edu

History Series -Sea Road Arts -Serial Number 002 Paper by David EP Dennis BA (Hons) FCIPD LCGI RAF Title: The Deep Roots of the NHS | David E P Dennis - Academia.edu).

Other references:

1911 Encyclopædia Britannica/Irnerius - Wikisource, the free online library

Dictionary of National Biography, 1885-1900/Vacarius - Wikisource, the free online library

Hannam (2009) *God's Philosophers: How the Medieval World Laid the Foundations of Modern Science*, UK: Icon Books.

https://medieval.yale.edu/people/marcia-colish

https://www.lawed.ie/guide-to-law-for-secondary-school-students-english-version/

Lockwood (2017) *The Conquest of Death – Violence and the Birth of the Modern English State*, London, Yale University Press.

Maxwell Lyte (1886) *A History of the University of Oxford – From The Earliest Times to the Year 1530*, London, Macmillan Press.

O'Callaghan (1975) *A History of Medieval Spain*, London, Cornell University Press.

Potter (2015) *Law, Liberty and the Constitution – A Brief History of the Common Law*, Woodbridge, The Boydell Press.

Reston (James Jr.) (2015) *Luther's Fortress – Martin Luther and His Reformation Under Siege*, new York, Basic Books.

Sager (2005) *Oxford & Cambridge – An Uncommon History*, London, Thames and Hudson.

Spearing (2002) (trans.) *The Cloud of Unknowing and Other Works*, London, Penguin Classics.

Taliadoros (2006) *Law and Theology in Twelfth-Century England: The Works of Master Vacarius (C.1115/1120-C.1200): 10 (Disputatio)*, Brepols N. V. and other works (2008) (2010)

See also:

Master Vacarius, civil lawyer, canon of Southwell and parson of Norwell, Nottinghamshire

Michael Jones p. 389-405 at Rennes University Press: **https://books.openedition.org/pur/141477?lang=en**

Chapter II

Dateline

Approximate Dates for the Relevant Events

BCE

384 - 322 – Aristotle

427 – 347 – Plato

4 – Jesus born

CE

33 – Jesus crucified

354 – Pelagius born. St Augustine of Hippo born

359 – Gratian of the Nicene Creed born

383 – Gratian of the Nicene Creed dies

418 – Pelagius dies

430 – St Augustine of Hippo dies

482 – Emperor Justinian born

565 – Emperor Justinian dies

1050 – Irnerius of Lombardy born

1070 – First Bologna lectures on Roman jurisprudence by Pepo

1084 onwards – Irnerius starts the School of Glossators

1088 – Formation of Bologna learning community

1090 – St Bernard of Clairvaux born

1096 – Oxford learning community exists

1115 – Roger of Pont L'Eveque born

1116 – Irnerius taken into court of Emperor Henry V

1118 – King Henry I Law Book – *Leges Henrici Primi* finalised after starting in 1115

1119 – Thomas Becket born

1120 – Vacarius born

1121 – First trial of Peter Abelard

1125 – Hugh de Puiset born

1126 – Irnerius – date of death? Or 1140

1135 – King Stephen begins rule

1138 – Theobald , Abbot of Bec becomes Archbishop of Canterbury

1139 – Lateran Council

1140 – Gratian the Monk of Bologna clarifies canon law. Second trial of Peter Abelard

1143 – Vacarius comes to Oxford? Thomas Becket in Rome to see Pope Celestine

1149 – Vacarius makes detailed civil law extracts from Code of Justinian

1153 – St Bernard of Clairvaux dies

1154 – King Stephen dies. Thomas Becket in Bologna,

Stephen Langton – soon to be an Archbishop, is born

1155 – Thomas Becket made Lord Chancellor

1158 – Gratian the Monk dies. University of Bologna given Imperial privileges.

1161 – Archbishop Theobald of Bec dies

1162 – Thomas Becket becomes a priest and then next day becomes Archbishop of Canterbury

1163 – King Henry rules

1164 – Vacarius in Paris

1166 – Assize of Clarendon. John, soon to be King John, is born

1167 – Oxford students return from University of Paris

1170 – Thomas Becket assassinated

1170 – 1180 – Vacarius teaches at Lincoln

1171 – Vacarius in Aumale

1175 – Vacarius in Norfolk

1176 – King Henry II orders the General Eyre

1179 – Grand Assizes ordered

1181- Robert of Pont L'Eveque dies

1189 – Law Book *Glanville* completed after starting in 1187

1194 – King Richard I institutes the Office of the Coroner

1195 – Hugh de Puiset dies

1198 – Last mention of Vacarius

1200 – Probably death date of Vacarius

1207 – Henry III (Henry Winchester) born

1200 – University of Paris given status by King of France

1201 – Oxford's first chancellor

1210 – Aristotle's philosophy books banned in Paris

1214 – Friar Roger Bacon born

1216 – King John dies. Henry III crowned

1219 – Last record of a trail by Ordeal

1220 – Henry III re-crowned. First record of a criminal jury trial

1228 – Archbishop Stephen Langton dies

1231 – Friar Roger Bacon of Oxford goes to Paris. The pope reinstates Aristotle's philosophy books

1237 – Roger Bacon lectures on Aristotle at University of Paris

1248 – Oxford's first royal charter from Henry III

1257 – Thomas Aquinas becomes a Doctor of Theology in Paris

1265 – John Duns Scotus born

1268 – Roger Bacon completes great works for the pope

1272 – Henry III dies

1274 – Thomas Aquinas dies

1275 – Marsilius of Padua born

1277 – Young Duns Scotus at Oxford. The Bishop of Paris condemns the writing of Averroes and Thomism (Aquinas)

1290 – Thomas Bradwardine – the Oxford polymath is born

1292 – Friar Roger Bacon dies

1300 – William of Ockham (Occam) enters Oxford University. Formal instruction in common law and statutes for 'apprentices of the bench'

1308 – John Dun Scotus dies

1309 – The pope moves to Avignon

1320 – Ockham gains his degree and leaves Oxford. Bradwardine enters Merton College, Oxford

1323 – Thomas Aquinas made a saint. Bradwardine obtains his degree as Master of Theology

1325 – Bradwardine is proctor of Oxford University

1327 – Cecco d'Ascoli burnt in Florence (philosopher/astrologer)

1328 – John Wycliffe born

1339 – Bradwardine appointed chaplain and confessor to Edward III. Authorities in Paris try to ban the works of William of Ockham

1343 – Marsilius of Padua dies

1347 – Black Death arrives in Europe

1348 – Black Death arrives in England. Bradwardine appointed Archbishop of Canterbury

1349 – Bradwardine confirmed by Avignon pope as Archbishop of Canterbury on 19th July but dies on month later (26 August) as Lambeth Palace

1366 – Camera Stellata (Star Chamber) named after being built in 1348

1369 – Jan Hus born

1377 – Two popes, one at Rome and one at Avignon.

Western Schism

1384 – John Wycliffe dies

1401 – *De heretic comburendo* – the burning of heretics - legislation passed in England

1415 – Jan Hus burnt for heresy

1428 – John Wycliffe's body dug up, burnt and thrown into River Swift

1513 – The Roman Catholic Church claims that it can unerringly prove the immortality of the soul using philosophical arguments

1517 – Martin Luther's decides that enough is enough and his 95 theses are nailed to the door in Wittenburg – setting off the great Reformation

1535 – Oxford University abolishes the medieval syllabus

1886 – History of Oxford University published (Maxwell Lyte)

1917 – Some canon law modified

1983 – Canon law codified officially

Chapter 12

Other books by David EP Dennis

<u>**History Genre – Published**</u>

Mysteries of Sussex Volume 1 ISBN-10 1872889395

Mysteries of Sussex Volume 2 ISBN-10 1872889417

Notes & Queries Volume 1 ISBN-10 1872889409

Notes & Queries Volume 2 ISBN-10 1872889425

The History of Old Winchelsea –

ISBN-13: 979-8223316343

<u>**To be published soon:**</u>

<u>**Medieval Oxford Series**</u>

Volume 2 – The Attempted Assassination of King Henry III

<u>**History Genre – to be published soon**</u>

History of Fore Wood, Crowhurst, Sussex

Richard the Lionheart and the London Riot – 1196

Historical Fantasy

The Saga of Calum the Dove (to be published shortly)

Academic Papers by David EP Dennis BA (Hons) FCIPD LCGI RAF

David E P Dennis | Independent Researcher - Academia.edu

www.ingramcontent.com/pod-product-compliance
Lightning Source LLC
LaVergne TN
LVHW090426210926
848480LV00002B/699